*Maureen Sinclair's*

# GAMES
# A
# BOGIE

SEANACHAIDH PUBLISHING LTD
Greenock, Scotland PA15 1BT
1989

# SEANACHAIDH PUBLISHING LTD
Greenock, Scotland PA15 1BT
## 1989

Printed by: Holmes MacDougall, Glasgow.

Photographs by: Elizabeth Cairns.

## ISBN: 0 948963 45 X

# CONTENTS

## GLASGOW LAMENT

Oh where is the Glasgow where I used to stay?
With white wally closes done up with pipe clay,
Where you knew every neighbour from first floor to third
And to keep your door shut was considered absurd.

And where are the weans that once played in the street?
Wi' a jorrie, a peerie, a grid wi' a cleet
Can they still cadge a hudgie, or dreep aff a dyke?
Play hunch cuddy hunch, kick the can and the like.

And where is the wee shop where I used to buy
A quarter o' tatties, a tuppenny pie?
A bag o' broke biscuits, a wee sodie scone,
And the wummin aye asked, 'How's yer maw gettin' oan'

Where is the tallies that I knew so well?
That wee corner chippy where they used to sell
Hot peas, a McCallum, ice cream in a poke,
you knew they were tallies the minute they spoke.

And where is the cludgie, that cosy wee cell?
The string frae the cistern – I remember it well
Where I sat wi' a caun'le and studied the nags
A win fur the Celtic, a defeat fur the Jags.

And where is the tram car that once did a ton
Doon the Great Western Road on the loe Yoker run?
The conductress aye knew how to deal wi' the nyaff,
If yer gaun well come oan, if yer no well get aff.

1

I think o' the days o' my tenement hame
We've got fancy hooses but they're just no' the same.
I'll swap your gizunders, flyovers and jams
For a tuppenny ride on the old Partick trams.

Gone is the Glesga that I used to know
Big Wullie, wee Shooie, the steamie, the Co.
The Shilpit wee bachle, the glaikit big dreep,
Yer baws oan the slates and her gas at a peep.

Those days were'ny rosie and money was tight,
The wages hauf finished by Saturday night.
But still we came through it and weathered the ruts,
The reason is simple – oor parents had guts.

Most street games had rules and regulations in common. The words and phrases listed below had the same meanings whichever game was being played.

HET – A person who is 'het' is the one who is elected to seek out or catch the others in certain games.

DEN – This is the place where the game usually starts and finishes and where any decisions regarding the current game are made.

KEYS – This is the word spoken by someone (usually holding his two thumbs up) whenever he wishes to say something to whoever is 'het' without having to stop the game or be caught.

OUT – A person is 'out' if he has been beaten or caught in a game.

IN – A person is 'in' if he hasn't been beaten or caught in a game.

THE GAME'S A BOGIE, THE MAN IN THE LOBBIE, COME OOT, COME OOT, WHEREVER YE ARE! –This verse is chanted whenever a game is to be stopped abruptly (usually when someone has cheated) and everyone must come out of hiding and return to the 'den'!

## ALEAVIO or RELEASE

This game is played with an equal number of players on each side. The team who are 'HET' have to chase and catch the members of the opposite team and bring them back to the 'DEN'. Someone from the 'HET' team usually stands guard at the 'DEN'. If someone from the other team runs through the 'DEN' without being caught and calls out "Aleavio" or "Release" all the prisoners are freed. The game continues until the whole team have been captured and brought back to the 'DEN'. The roles are then reversed.

## DODGIE BALL

One person is 'HET' and has to hit all the others with a ball below the knee. The object of the game is to avoid being hit by the ball and to stay in the game as long s possible. Once a person has been hit he is 'OUT'. The last person to be hit with the ball gets the privilege of being 'HET' in the next game.

## HIDE AND SEEK

Everyone runs off to hide while the person who is 'HET' stays in the 'DEN' and counts to an agreed number with his eyes closed. He must then seek everyone out and bring them back to the 'DEN'. When he finds someone he must call out the persons name, run back to the 'DEN' and shout "1, 2, 3". If the person who has been found reaches the 'DEN' first and call out "1, 2, 3" he wont's be 'out'. The game restarts and the 'HET' person will be whoever was found first in the previous game.

## O'GRADY SAYS

One person is O'Grady and gives rapid orders to the others by saying, "O'Grady says do this" e.g. clapping his hands or touching his toes and so on. Everyone must do what O'Grady does. But if he says "O'Grady says do that" and anyone does so, he is 'out'. The game goes on until there is only one person left and he gets to be O'Grady.

## WHAT'S THE TIME MR. WOLF?

'Mr. Wolf walks a few paces in front of the others and they walk slowly behind him saying, "What's the time Mr. Wolf?" He may turn round to them and say "It's 10 o'clock" or "it's 8 o'clock". But if he turns round and says "it's dinner time!" everyone must run back to the den without being caught by 'Mr. Wolf'. Anyone who is caught is 'out' and play continues until there is only one person left not caught by Mr. Wolf. He then becomes 'Mr. Wolf'.

## ALI BABA, ALI BABA, WHO'S GOT THE BALL?

One person stands with her back to the others and throws the ball far behind her. Someone retrieves it and everyone puts their hands behind their backs and chants, "Ali Baba, Ali Baba, who's got the ball? I haven't got it, in my pocket, I haven't got it at all." Whoever threw the ball has to guess who has it behind their back. If she guesses correctly she has another turn of throwing the ball. If she is wrong, then whoever retrieved the ball gets to throw it.

## STATUES

One person stands in the 'den' with her back to the others and counts to an agreed number. The other advance forward from the starting line. When the counting stops, they must not move. The person who is 'het' can try to make them laugh but must not touch them. If anyone moves, they must go back to the starting line. The process is repeated again and so on until someone reaches the 'den' without being seen moving. She is then 'het'.

## AUNTS AND UNCLES

One person stands in the 'den' and the others are a short distance away at the starting line. The person in the 'den' calls out the christian name of an aunt or uncle. If anyone has an aunt or uncle of that name they may take a step forward. If they have two or more aunts or uncles of that name, they may take two or more steps forward. Whoever reaches the 'den' first is the winner and takes a turn of calling.

# MR. CROCODILE

'Mr Crocodile' stands behind a line drawn with chalk on the ground. The others stand at the other side of the line and chant "Mr Crocodile, may we cross your waters?" He replies saying "not unless you have the colour blue on". or "not unless you had mince for your dinner". or something similar. Anyone who can satisfy his demand may cross the line, but the others have to make a dive for it and try not to let 'Mr Crocodile' catch them. Anyone who gets caught is 'out' and the game proceeds with a different demand from 'Mr Crocodile' each time. Whoever is last to be 'out' is the winner and he becomes 'Mr Crocodile'.

## HUNCH CUDDY HUNCH

Hunch cuddy hunch is played by two teams. The first team make a 'cuddy' by hunching over horse fashion. The first person stands with his back against the wall. The next person hunches over and holds on to him. The third does likewise and so on depending how many are in the team. The other team have to run and leap on to the 'cuddy' one by one. Once they have all mounted the 'cuddy' it starts to wriggle about trying to dismount everyone. The object is to try and stay on the the cuddy as long as possible. When everyone has been dismounted they must then become the cuddy.

## PIG IN THE MIDDLE

This game is played by three players. A ball is passed between two of the players and the third player must try to catch it, the person who missed his throw becomes the 'pig in the middle'.

## KICK THE CAN

This game is similar to hide and seek. An old tin can is kicked as far away as possible from the 'DEN' and whoever is 'HET' has to retrieve it while everone else runs off to hide. The object of the game is is to find everyone and bring them back to the 'DEN'. If someone who hasn't been caught manages to sneak back to the 'DEN' without being seen by 'HET' he can kick the can again and release everyone in the 'DEN' who has been caught. Once everyone has been caught the game begins again and the first person to be caught will be 'HET'.

# ROUNDERS

This game is played by two teams. A bat and ball are used and four circles called 'Dults' are drawn with chalk on the ground. The object of the game is to bat the ball and try to run a full circle passing through each of the 'dults' before the opposing team catch the ball and bounce it in to one of the 'dults'.

A player can stop to rest in one of the 'dults' if he knows he won't be able to complete a full round. He may complete his round when the next player takes his turn. If the opposing team bounce the ball in a 'dult' while a player is still running, then the player is out. His team mates must complete three full rounds before he can get back in the game.

If the opposing team catch the ball after it has been batted, without it having touched the ground, then the whole batting team are 'out' When everyone in the batting team are out, the opposing team take over, and the positions are reversed.

## POPULAR GIRLS' GAMES AND PASTIMES

There were 'seasons' for girls' games such as skipping ropes, balls, scraps, peever and crochet.
In the 'scraps season' the girls would collect picture scraps in the pages of an old paperback book and swap scraps with each other. This could go on for weeks and then it would be the turn of skipping ropes or balls. Although skipping ropes was traditionally a girl's game, sometimes the boys would join in 'for a laugh'. Some of them were far better at skipping than the girls. Then the season would change again to either peever or crochet. During the 'crochet season' the girls sat in groups and crocheted for all they were worth, trying to see who could make the largest mat. Usually the mats ended up so big that they were put into the beds in winter for extra warmth.

Other pastimes for girls included playing houses and shops. The houses were partitioned off with pieces of wood on the ground. They were furnished with discarded linoleum and cardboard and old orange boxes. The children would 'visit' each other for a 'cup of tea' and go to the 'shop' together. In the 'shop', old tin cans were filled with earth and the lids were bent over and used as scoops. Broken coloured glass was used as money and old newspapers were cut into squares and used as wrapping paper. The scales were pieces of cardboard with stones as weights.

## POPULAR BOYS' GAMES AND PASTIMES

Just as the girls had their favourite pastimes, so did the boys have theirs.

They had their whip and peerie, jorries (or marbles), gird and cleet, and of course, football.

A peerie was a type of spinning top which required a lot of skill to be able to spin it with a whip. They usually had patterns drawn on them with coloured chalk which gave out a nice effect when the peerie was spinning. The object of this game was to see whose peerie could spin the longest.

A gird was a large hoop, usually made of metal and a cleet was a thin bar with a loop at the end which hooked on to the gird. This was used to help to guide the gird along the street. Sometimes they would just use the hoop from an old barrel and a stick to guide it. They usually has races with their girds from one corner of the street to the next.

Jorries (or marbles) was another favourite with the boys. There were many variations of playing jorries, but the final object was always the same, and that was to win as many jorries as possible from your opponent.

Another pastime was to make things out of discarded items. A bogie (or cart) was made from some pieces of wood, old pram wheels, and a length of rope for steering. With a few nails and a hammer, who needed a Rolls Royce? Stilts were made from two empty tin cans with two holes pierced on the top of each. A length of string was threaded through the holes and tied and hey presto, a pair of stilts.

11

# SECTION 1

# STREET SONGS

## INTRODUCTION

Street games and songs were once the main source of recreation for many Glasgow and Scottish children.

Families were larger and money for toys was scarce, so owning a bike or a pram was a pipe dream for most. There were no clubs to go to and they usually played in and around the streets and back courts. They made there own entertainment by playing games and making up songs as they went along

Most of the songs they sang had a humourous side to them, though some hit on a more serious note. Whatever the theme, they had great fun singing them.

Yesterdays children may have been poor, but they were rich in laughter and imagination.

Ali bali ali bali bee
Sittin' on your mammy's knee
Greetin' for a wee bawbee
To buy some coulter's candy
Coulter's candy a penny a lump
That's the stuff to make you jump
If you jump you're sure to fall
Okey Cokey that's it all


Charlie Chaplin went to France
To teach the ladies how to dance
He swept the lassies aff their feet
While laughin' at his Chaplin feet


Charlie he belongs to the mill
The mill belongs to Charlie still
Charlie he belongs to the mill
The mill belongs to Charlie still


Clappa clappa handies
Daddy's comin' hame
Pennies in his pocket
For his ain wee wean


Dial 999 dial 999
Robert Beattie stole a sweetie
Dial 999

Don't do that to the wee pussycat
Do not hurt her so
Do not drive your friends away
You might be a pussycat yourself one day
So don't do that to the wee pussycat
No no no no no.


Hot peas and mutton pies
Tell me where ma Johnnie lies
I'll be there before he dies
To roll him in my bosom
Whit dae ye think o' my wee lad?
Whit dae ye think o' Johnnie?
Whit dae ye think o' my wee lad?
I think he's awfie bonnie.

How wid ye like tae be me?
How wid ye like tae be me?
A lump o' fat stuck in ma hat
How wid ye like tae be me?


I am Italian so brave and bold
So all alone dear, so all alone
I take my banjo upon my knee
I sing to you dear, sweet Genevieve
Sweet Genevieve, sweet Genevieve
Why don't you marry me, marry me
Cos I'm a poor wee wee Italian boy.
I have no mother
No father dear
No sister brother
To wipe my tear
To wipe my tear, to wipe my tear
Why don't you marry me, marry me
Cos I'm a poor wee Italian boy.


I know where I'm goin'
An' I know who's goin wi' me
I've got a laud o' ma ain
An' they call him Bonnie Jimmie
Jimmie wears a kilt
He wears it in a fashion
An' every time he burls aroon
Ye canni help fur laughin'.

If you should see a big fat wummin
Standing at the corner bummin'
That's ma mammy.
If you should see her wearin' glasses
Smiling at each one that passes
That's ma mammy.


I'm a poor little orphan girl
My mother she is dead
My father is a drunkard
And won't give me my bread
I peep through the window
I hear the organ play
God bless my dear old mother
For she is far away
Ding dong the castle bell
Farewell to my mother
Bury me in the old church yard
Beside my elder brother
My coffin shall be white
Six little angels by my side
Two to play and two to say
And two to carry my soul away.


Jenny Myer blow the fire
Puff puff puff
When she sits on husband's knee
Snuff snuff snuff
When she goes to bed at night
Huff huff huff.

I married a wife oh then, oh then
I married a wife oh then, oh then
I married a wife
And she hit me with a knife
Oh the world must be coming to an end

I sent her for butter oh then, oh then
I sent her for butter oh then, oh then
I sent her for butter
And she fell in the gutter
Oh the world must be coming to an end

I sent her for cheese oh then, oh then
I sent her for cheese oh then, oh then
I sent her for cheese And she fell and skint her
knee
Oh the world must be coming to an end

I sent her for bread oh then, oh then
I sent her for bread oh then, oh then
I sent her for bread
And she dropped doon dead
Oh the world must be coming to an end.


I say what a smasher
No woodbine — only pasha.


Last night ah got an awfie hammerin'
Who frae? Frae wee Georgie Cameron
Whit fur? Fur callin' his daddy greasy beard
I'll tell the bobbies in the mornin'.

I once had a dear old mother
Who was very kind to me
And when I had some troubles
She sat me on her knee
One night as I lay sleeping
Upon my tiny bed
An angel came from heaven
An told me mother was dead
I woke up in the morning
To see if this was true
Yes mother was up in heaven
Above the sky so blue
Now children obey your parents
And do as you are told
For when you lose your mother
You lose a heart of gold.


Kiltie kiltie cauld bum
Three stairs up
The wummin in the middle door
Hit him wi' a cup
The cup was full o' jelly
She hit him in the belly
Kiltie kiltie cauld bum
Three stairs up.


No' last night but the night before
Three wee beggars came to ma door
One had a fiddle, one had a drum
And one had a pancake stuck to his bum.

Last night ah went tae the pictures
Ah took a front seat at the back
Ah fell frae the pit tae the gallery
An broke the front bone at the back
A wummin she gave me some chocolates
Ah ate them an' gave her them back
She said ah wis comin' on funny
An' gave me a big lassie slap.


Last night there wis murder in the fish shop
A wee dug stole a haddie bone
A big dug tried tae get it aff him
So ah hit him wi' a big tattie scone
Ah shouted on ma auntie Sarah
Ma auntie Sarah wisnae in
Ah peeped through a hole in the windae
An' ah shouted 'auntie Sarah, are ye in?'
Her teeth were lyin' on the table
Her hair wis hangin' oot the bed
Ah nearly burst ma sides wi' laughin'
When ah saw her screwin' aff her wooden leg.


Ma faither died a month ago
An' left me a' his riches
A feather bed, a wooden leg
An' a pair o' leather breeches
A coffee pot without a spout
A cup without a handle
A baccy box without a lid
An hauf a ha'penny candle.

Ma wee laud's a sodjer
He works in Maryhill
He gets his pay on a Friday night
An' buys a hauf a gill
He goes tae church on Sunday
A half an hour late
He pulls the buttons aff his shirt
An' puts them in the plate.


Murder, murder polis
Three stairs up
The wummin in the middle door
Hit me wi' a cup
Ma head's a' blood
An' ma face is a' cut
Murder, murder polis
Three stairs up
Send fur the doctor
The doctor widnae come
Send fur the ambulance
Run, run, run.


Me an' ma granny an' a whole lot mair
Kicked up a rammy on the wash hoose stair
Alang came a polisman  and said 'Who's there?'
Jist me an' ma granny an' a whole lot mair.

Ma mammy says tae me
Wid ye like a cup o' tea
Ah says no, no, Ah like cocoa
Down in the glen
She took me by the hand
All the way to Barrowland
Ah says no, no, Ah like cocoa
Down in the glen.


Ma maw's a millionaire
Wid ye believe it?
Blue eyes an' curly hair
Wid ye believe it?
Sittin' among the eskimoes
Playin' a game o' dominoes
Ma maw's a millionaire.


One two three, ma mammy caught a flea
She put it in her sugar bowl
And took it to her tea

One two three, ma mammy caught a flea
She roasted it, she toasted it
And took it to her tea

One two three, ma mammy caught a flea
She put it in the frying pan
And fried it for her tea.

My name is Biggar
But Ah wis born wee
Ma name is Biggar
But bigger Ah'll never be
Though Ah'm only four feet four
Ah'll no' tell a lie
Although ma name is Biggar
Ah'll be wee until Ah die.


Mary, oh Mary are ye no' comin' oot?
Yer laud's at the corner
He's walkin' aboot
His haun's in his pockets
His shirt's hangin' oot
Mary, oh Mary are ye no' comin' oot?
Mary, oh Mary, oh Mary come quick
Yer laud's wi' the polis
He's goin' tae the nick
He stole three rolls
As hard as a brick
Mary, oh Mary, oh Mary come quick.


Down yonder green valley
I met a wee tali
He gave me some biscuits
To start a wee shop
Before the shop started
The wee tali farted
And blew a' ma biscuits
Away up a kye.

Ma uncle Tam frae Glesca cam
Alang wi' ma Auntie Jenny
He said he'd gie me somethin' nice
An' he gied me a braw new penny
Ah went an' bought some candy rock
Alang wi' Jimmy A'Hara
Ah gied him a lick o' ma liquorice stick
Fur a shot o' his wee barra
Oh the bonnie wee barra's mine
It disnae belang tae A'Hara
The fly wee bloke — he stuck tae ma rock
So Ah'm gonni stick tae his barra.


Ma maw says Ah've tae go
Wi' ma faither's dinner-o
Champit totties, stewin' steak
An' a wee bit currant cake
Ah came tae a river
Ah couldnae get across
Ah paid ten bob fur an auld scabby horse
Ah jumped on his back
His bones gave a crack
Ah had tae wait till the boat came back
The boat came back
We a' jumped in
The boat capsized
An' we a' fell in
Singing don't be weary
Try an' be cheery
Don't be weary
Cos we're a' gaun hame.

My eyes are dim I cannot see
I have not brought my specs with me
I have not brought my specs with me

There was cheese, cheese
As hard as Hitler's knees
In the store, in the store
There was cheese, cheese
As hard as Hitler's knees
In the quartermaster's stores

My eyes are dim I cannot see
I have not brought my specs with me
I have not brought my specs with me

There was ham, ham
That wisnae worth a damn
In the store, in the store
There was ham, ham
That wisnae worth a damn
In the quartermaster's store

My eyes are dim I cannot see
I have not brought my specs with me
I have not brought my specs with me.


Coco Bendy had a wife
She was awfie dandy
She fell in beneath the bed
And tumbled o'er the chanty
Coco Bendy he came in
And smelt an awfie stink
He went in beneath the bed
And had a fizzy drink.

One two three a-leary
Haud ma whip tae a spin ma peerie
Oh Ah canni spin ma peerie
Ah wish Ah wis a wee laudie.

One two three, ma mammy caught a flea
She put it in the sugar bowl
And took it to her tea

One two three, ma mammy caught a flea
She roasted it, she toasted it
And took it to her tea

One two three, ma mammy caught a flea
She put it in the frying pan
And fried it for her tea.


One fine day in the middle of the night
Two dead men got up to fight
Back to back they faced each other
Drew out a sword and shot each other.


One two three o-leary
I saw Wallace Beary
Sitting on his bum-ba-leerie
Kissing Shirley Temple.


Ha ha ha hee hee hee
Three wee monkies up a tree
One fell doon and hurt his knee
Ha ha ha hee hee hee

Once I had a wee bit hen
It had a wee bit lean
I sent it for an ounce o' snuff
It never came back again
I'll hae a funeral fur ma wee hen
I'll hae a funeral fur ladies and gentlemen
Ladies and Gentlemen, bless ma wee hen
God bless ma wee hen
Will never come back again.


Open the pub fur Geordie
Open the pub fur Geordie
He's staunin ootside
So open it wide
Open the pub fur Geordie.


Paddy on the railway
Picking up stones
Along came an engine
And broke Paddy's bones
Oh says Paddy 'That's no' fair'
Oh says the engine man
'Ye shouldnae hae been there'.


Oh Peter the Taliman
Chippie no' ready
Wait a wee minute
I'll no' be long.

Oor wee school's the best wee school
The best wee school in Glesca
The only thing that's wrang wi' it
Is the baldy heided master
He goes tae the pub on a Saturday night
He goes tae the church on Sunday
he prays to God to gie him strength
Tae belt the weans on Monday.


Pity on the river
Pity on the brook
Pity on the one
Who steals this book
When you die God will say
Where is the book you stole away
If you say I do not know
God will send you down below.


Does yer maw drink wine
Does she drink it a' the time
Does she ever get the feelin'
That she's gonni hit the ceilin'
Does yer maw drink wine?

Does yer maw drink gin
Does she drink it oot a tin
Does she ever get the feelin'
That she's gonni hit the ceilin'
Does yer maw drink gin?

Doh ray me when Ah wis wee
Ah used to peel the totties
Noo Ah'm big an' Ah can jig
An' Ah can play wi' the laudies
Ma faither bought me a wee wee hoose
To keep me away frae the laudies
The hoose fell in
An' Ah fell oot
An' Ah fell in wi' the laudies.


Eight o'clock the bells are ringing
Mother let me out
My sweetheart is waiting for to take me out
He's going to give me apples
He's going to give me pears
He's going to give me kisses
Underneath the stairs


God bless the man
The man that invented sleep
There ought to be a monument
His memory to keep
We don't know his name
Nor we don't know his aim
But goodness we are just now realising
But oh by jingers
I would like to get my fingers
On the son of a gun of man
That invented early rising

Greasy beard a penny a yerd
A ha'penny a wee bit longer


Sixteen sums and what do you get
All of them wrong and none of them right
Oh teacher don't you call me cos I can't come
I'm stuck to ma seat with bubbly gum.


Sticks and stones will break my bones
But names will never hurt me
When you're dead and in your grave
You'll be sorry for what you called me.


Sugarally watter
Black as the lum
A' get a pin
And we'll a' get some.


The bell, the bell, the B-E-L
Tell the teacher I'm no' well
If yer late, shut the gate
The bell, the bell, the B-E-L.


Ye canni catch me fur a wee bawbee
Ha ha ha, hee hee hee.

This is the tree that never grew
This is the bird that never flew
This is the fish that never swam
This is the bell that never rang.


The boy stood on the burning deck
When all but he had fled
He tried to keep his trousers on
By standing on his head
The boy stood on the burning deck
His feet were covered with blisters
The fire burnt his trousers off
So he put on his sister's.


The minister in the pulpit
Couldnae say his prayers
He laughed an' he giggled
An' he fell doon the stairs
The stairs gave a crack
An' he broke his humphy back
An' a' the congregation
Went 'quack, quack, quack'.


The moon shines bright on Charlie Chaplin
His boots are crackin'
For the want o' blackin'
And his wee baggy troosers
Are needing mending
Before they send him to Dardanelles.

The weans have gone to Balloch
Wi' ribbons in their hair
To the bonnie banks of Loch Lomond
Dear God we'll all be there
Teacher, dear teacher,
Do you know what I have done?
My pastries fell into Loch Lomond
Will you give me another wee bun, bun, bun
I'll remember St. Patrick's excursion
Until I'm a hundred and one, one, one.


Tramp, tramp, tramp
The boys are marching
Tramp, tramp, tramp
They're off to war
Then we'll buy a penny gun
And make the Germans run
And we'll never see the Kaiser any more.


Up an' doon the hoose
Tae catch a mickey moose
If ye catch it by the tail
Hang it up on a rusty nail
Send for the cook
Tae make a bowl o' soup
Hurrah boys, hurrah boys
How d'ye like ma soup
Ah like it very well
But only for the smell
Hurrah boys, hurrah boys
How d'ye like ma soup.

They say that in the army
The fags are mighty fine
Ye ask fur twenty Capstan
They gie ye five Woodbine
Oh I just want to leave the army life
Gee boys, I want to go home
To see ma mammy
Gee boys, I want to go home

They say that in the army
The booze is mighty fine
Ye ask fur a bottle o' whiskey
They gie ye turpentine
Oh I just want to leave the army life
Gee boys, I wany to go home
To see ma mammy
Gee boys, I want to go home.


V for victory, dot dot dash
Hitler lost his wee moustache
If you find it, never mind it
V for victory, dot dot dash.


V for victory, dot dot dash
Hitler lost his wee moustache
When he fun it, he lost his bunnet
V for victory, dot dot dash.

Wee chookie birdie toh loh loh
Laid an egg on the windae soll
The windae soll began to crack
Wee chookie birdie, quack quack quack.


Two wee craws sat upon a wa'
Sat upon a wa', sat upon a wa'
Two wee craws sat upon a wa'
On a cold and frosty morning

The first wee craw couldnae fly at a'
Couldnae fly at a', couldnae fly at a'
The first wee craw couldnae fly at a'
On a cold and frosty morning

The second wee craw wis greetin' fur his maw
Greetin' fur his maw, greetin' fur his maw
The second wee craw wis greetin' fur his maw
On a cold and frosty morning

The third wee craw wisnae there at a'
Wisnae there at a', wisnae there at a'
The third wee craw wisnae there at a'
On a cold and frosty morning.


Wee Annie's a smasher
A face like a tottie masher
A nose like a pickled onion
And big smelly feet.

When Ah wis single
Ah used tae powder puff
Noo that Ah'm married
Ah havnae got the stuff
It's a life, a life
A weary, weary life
It's better tae be single
Than tae be a married wife

Wan says 'Daddy, gie's a piece on jam'
Another says 'Mammy, hurl me in ma pram'
It's a life, a life
A weary, weary life
It's better tae be single
Than tae be a married wife

Wan says 'Daddy, put me in tae bed'
Another says 'Mammy, scratch ma wooden leg'
It's a life, a life
A weary, weary life
It's better tae be single
Than tae be a married wife.

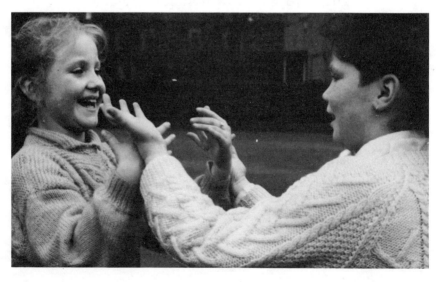

Ye canni shove yer granny aff a bus
Ye canni shove yer granny aff a bus
Ye canni shove yer granny
Cos she's yer mammy's mammy
Ye canni shove yer granny aff a bus

Ye can shove yer other granny aff a bus
Ye can shove yer other granny aff a bus
Ye can shove yer other granny
Cos she's yer daddy's mammy
Ye can shove yer other granny aff a bus


Ye red heided sinner
Come up fur yer dinner
Cauld totties an' herrin'


Whit's yer name?
Baldy Bain
Stick yer nose in an aeroplane
An' don't come back tae me again.


Hey Jock ma cuddy
Ma cuddy's o'er the dyke
An' if ye touch ma cuddy
Ma cuddy'll gie ye a bite.

Hallelujah slice the dumpling
Hallelujah amen
Hallelujah slice the dumpling
Hallelujah amen.


Skinny malinky long legs
Big banana feet
Went to the pictures
And couldnae find a seat
When the picture started
Skinny malinky farted
Skinny malinky long legs
Big banana feet.


Taffy was a Welsh man
Taffy was a thief
Taffy came tae ma hoose
An' stole a lump o' beef
Ah went tae Taffy's hoose
Taffy wisnae in
Taffy came tae ma hoose
An' stole a rollin' pin
Ah went tae Taffy's hoose
Taffy wis in bed
Ah got the rollin' pin
An' threw it at his head.

My heart is as light as a feather
I hope it will never grow sad
I'm going to be married tomorrow
But not to that ugly show-off

That ugly show-off is deceitful
He's always smoking a pipe
He's always kissing the lassies
Especially on Saturday night

Don't speak to me any more
I'm quite a lady passing by your door
Your hair won't curl
Nor your boots won't shine
You're not nice looking
So you won't be mine

See that fellow how he winks his eye
He thinks I love him
But he's telling a lie

Haw Sammy yer face is awfie jammy
Away and tell yer mammy
Tae wash it aff.


Tommy Morgan had an organ
And his father had a drum
And his sister had a blister
On the corner of her bum.


Peery weery winkle
I saw your wee twinkle
Peery weery winkle
You never saw mine.

Tell tale tit yer mammy canni knit
Yer daddy canni go tae work
Without a walking stick

Tell tale tit yer mammy canni knit
Yer daddy canni go tae bed
without a dummy tit.

I am a brownie dressed in brown
See my knickers hanging down
Pull them up, pull them down
I am a brownie dressed in brown.

Wee MacGreegor he's like a neegir
His name was even on the Irn Bru
He wears a tammy, tae please his mammy
Oh MacGreegor, greegor, greegor, greegor do.

Felix had a baby
Had a baby boy
He wis like his daddy
They only called him Paddy
Paddy died and Felix cried
And all the people laughed
Ha ha ha, hee hee hee
Three wee monkeys up a tree
But he kept on walking
He kept on walking still.


I'm no' hairy Mary I'm yer maw
I'm no' hairy Mary I'm yer maw
I'm no' hairy Mary, I'm no' hairy Mary
I'm no' hairy Mary I'm yer maw


It's raining, it's pouring
And Hitler said to Goering
I've lost my pants
In the middle of France
And I can't fight the British
This morning.


Kiltie kiltie cauld bum
Couldnae play a drum
He lifted up his petticoat
And showed his dirty bum
His dirty bum was dirty
He showed it to the queen
The queen was disappointed
And jagged it wi' a peen.

## SECTION 2

## CIRCLE GAMES

## INTRODUCTION

A group of children formed a circle and sang and acted out the words of a rhyme.

Sometimes one child would go in to the centre of the circle and do the actions, whilst the others clapped their hands and sang the song.

When the rhyme ended, the child in the centre would choose someone else to take her place and either the rhyme would be sung again or a new one would be started.

Ali baba ali baba who's got the ball?
I haven't got it in my pocket
I haven't got it at all.


Bee baw babbity, babbity, babbity
bee baw babbity
A lassie or a wee laudie o
Ah widnae hae a lassie o
A lassie o, a lassie o
Ah widnae hae a lassie o
Ah'd rather hae a wee laudie.


There was a farmer had a dog
His name was Bobby Bingo
B–I–N–G–O B–I–N–G–O
B–I–N–G–O
His name was Bobby Bingo.


Bobby Shaftoe's gone to sea
Silver buckles on his knee
He'll come back and marry me
Bonny Bobby Shaftoe

Bobby Shaftoe's bright and fair
Combing down his yellow hair
He's my ain for ever mair
Bonnie Bobby Shaftoe.

Here we go round the mulberry bush
The mulberry bush, the mulberry bush
Here we go round the mulberry bush
On a cold and frosty morning

This is the way we wash our hands
Wash our hands, wash our hands
This is the way we wash our hands
On a cold and frosty morning

Here we go round the mulberry bush etc.

This is the way we wash our face
Wash our face, wash our face
This is the way we wash our face
On a cold and frosty morning

Here we go round the mulberry bush etc.

This is the way we brush our teeth
Brush our teeth, brush our teeth
This is the way we brush our teeth
On a cold and frosty morning

Here we go round the mulberry bush etc.

This is the way we comb our hair
Comb our hair, comb our hair
This is the way we comb our hair
On a cold and frosty morning

Here we go round the mulberry bush etc.

Chorus; Here we go looby loo
             Here we go looby light
             Here we go looby loo
             All on a Saturday night

You put your right arm in
You put your right arm out
Shake it a little a little
And turn yourself about
Chorus
Your put your left arm in, etc.
Chorus
Youe put your right leg in, etc.
Chorus
You put your left leg in, etc.
Chorus
You put your whole self in, etc.
Chorus.


I am a little Dutch girl
I live in Holland
Holland is the land
Where we dance and sing
My shoes are made of wood
And my cosy stockings
Have so many colours
Sometimes red
Clat clatter clat clatter
Tiny little shoes, shoes
Clat clatter clat clatter
Tiny little shoes.

I'm a bow legged chicken
I'm a knock kneed hen
Haven't been so happy
Since I don't know when
I walk with a wiggle
And a giggle and a gog
Doing the Tennessee Wig Wog
Put your toes together
Your knees apart
Bend your back
Get ready to start
Flap your elbows just for luck
Then you wiggle and you woggle
Like a baby duck.


I'm a girl guide all dressed in blue
These are the actions I must do
Stand at ease
Bend your knees
Quick march under the arch
Salute to the King
Bow to the Queen
And turn your back to the Kaiser.


A ring a ring o' roses
A pocket full of posies
Atishoo! atishoo!
We all fall down

I have a bonnet trimmed with blue
Do you wear it? Yes I do
I always wear it when I can
Going to the ball with my young man
My young man has gone to sea
When he comes back he will marry me
Tip to the heel
And tip to the toe
That's the way the polka goes.


I lost ma wee canary, canary, canary
I lost ma wee canary
A humpty dumpty doo
I'll need to buy another one, another one
another one
I'll need to but another one
A humpty dumpty doo
I met her in a dance hall
A dance hall, a dance hall
I met her in a dance hall
A humpty dumpty doo
This is the one that I love
I love, I love
This is the one that I love
A humpty dumpty doo
Red cheeks and roses, roses, roses
Red cheeks and roses
A humpty dumpty doo.

I'm a little Dutch girl
A Dutch girl, a Dutch girl
I'm a little Dutch girl
A Dutch girl am I

I'm a little Dutch boy
A Dutch boy, a Dutch boy
I'm a little Dutch boy
A Dutch boy am I

Oh see my pretty apron
My apron, my apron
Oh see my pretty apron
My apron I wear

Oh see my baggy trousers
Baggy trousers, baggy trousers
Oh see my baggy trousers
Baggy trousers I wear

See my pretty necklace
My necklace, my necklace
Oh see my pretty necklace
My necklace I wear

Oh give me that necklace
That necklace, that necklace
Oh give me that necklace
That necklace you wear

Oh go away I hate you
I hate you, I hate you
Oh go away I hate you
I hate you I do

Oh why do you hate me
You hate me, you hate me
Oh why do you hate me
You hate me do you

Because you stole my necklace
My necklace, my necklace
Because you stole my necklace
My necklace I wore

Oh please will you forgive me
Forgive me, forgive me
Oh please will you forgive me
Forgive me, will you?

Then we shall get married,
Get married, get married
Then we shall get married
Get married, we shall

And then we'll have a baby
A baby, a baby
And then we'll have a baby
A baby we'll have

I'm a sailor home from sea
To see if you will marry me
If you will marry arry arry arry
If you will marry me

So you're a sailor home from sea
To see if you can marry me
Well I won't marry arry arry arry
I won't marry you

I will give you a bouncing ball
That bounces from the kitchen into the hall
If you will marry arry arry arry
If you will marry me

I don't want a bouncing ball
That bounces from the kitchen into the hall
And I won't marry arry arry arry
I won't marry you

I will give you a silver spoon
To feed your baby in the afternoon
If you will marry arry arry arry
If you will marry me

I don't want a silver spoon
To feed my baby in the afternoon
And I won't marry arry arry arry
I won't marry you

I will give you the keys of the chest
And all the money that I possess
If you will marry arry arry arry
If you will marry me

I will take the keys of the chest
And all the money that you possess
But I'll not marry arry arry arry
I'll not marry you

Ha ha ha you're awful funny
You don't want me but you want my money
Well I'll not marry arry arry arry
I'll not marry you!


In and out of the windows
In and out of the windows
In and out of the windows
As we have done before

I'll tell the bobby
I'll tell the bobby
I'll tell the bobby
As we have done before

Sixty days in prison
Sixty days in prison
Sixty days in prison
As we have done before

Hard bread and water
Hard bread and water
Hard bread and water
As we have done before

In and out those dusty bluebells
In and out those dusty bluebells
In and out those dusty bluebells
I am the master

Tipper ipper apper on my shoulders
Tipper ipper apper on my shoulders
Tipper ipper apper on my shoulders
I am the master

Follow me the master said
Follow me the master said
Follow me the master said
I am the master.


I saw a gypsy riding, riding, riding
I saw a gypsy riding, Y-O-U
What are you riding here for, here for, here for
What are you riding here for? Y-O-U
I'm riding here to marry, marry, marry
I'm riding here to marry, Y-O-U
And who are you going to marry, marry, marry
Who are you going to marry? Y-O-U
I'm going to marry you sir, you sir, you sir
I'm going to marry you sir, Y-O-U
I wouldn't marry you hen, you hen, you hen
I wouldn't marry you hen, Y-O-U
Why won't you marry me sir, me sir, me sir
Why won't you marry me sir? Y-O-U
Your face is so black and dirty, dirty, dirty
Your face is so black and dirty, Y-O-U

I sent a letter to my love
And on the way I dropped it
I dropped it once
I dropped it twice
I dropped it three times over
Over, over, in and out the clover
Over, over, in and out the clover.


I've got the legs like Betty Grable
I've got the figure like Marilyn Monroe
I've got the hair like Ginger Rodgers
And the face I do not know
I've got the eyes like Charlie Chaplin
They shine for you alone
Yes, I've got the legs like Betty Grable
And the figure like Marilyn Monroe.


Keep the sunny side up, up
And the other side, one, two
See those soldiers marching along
See those soldiers singing their song
Bend down and touch your toes
Just like the eskimoes
Bend down and touch your shins
Just like the Indians
Bend down and touch your knees
Just like the Japanese
And keep the sunny side up.

Mother went out to post a letter
Mother went out to post a letter
Mother went out to post a letter
Early in the morning.

She fell in with a drunken sailor
She fell in with a drunken sailor
She fell in with a drunken sailor
Early in the morning.

What shall we do with the drunken sailor?
What shall we do with the drunken sailor?
What shall we do with the drunken sailor?
Early in the morning.

Put him in the boat and roll him over
Put him in the boat and roll him over
Put him in the boat and roll him over
Early in the morning

The boat goes too slow, too slow, too slow
The boat goes too slow
Cock a leary – o
The boat goes too fast, too fast, too fast
The boat goes too fast
Cock a leary – o.


I'm Shirley Temple
And I've got curly hair
I've got dimples
And I wear my clothes to there
I'm not yet able
To do the Betty Grable
But I'm Shirley Temple
And I've got curly hair.

My girl's a corker
She's a New Yorker
I'd give her anything
To keep her in style
She's got a pair of legs
Just like two boiled eggs
That's where all my money goes
Oompah oompah oompah pah
Oompah pah, oompah pah
Oompah oompah oompah pah
That's where all my money goes.


My mummy told me if I was goody
That she would buy me a rubber dolly
But auntie told her
I kissed a soldier
Now she won't buy me a rubber dolly
Three six nine the goose drank wine
The monkey chewed tobacco
On the street car line
The line broke, the monkey got choked
And we all went to heaven in a little row boat.


Queen of Sheba, Queen of Sheba
Has lost her gold ring,
Lost her gold ring
Queen of Sheba, Queen of Sheba
Has lost her gld ring
Guess who has found it?

Nellie McSwiggan got tossed oot the jiggin'
For liftin' her leg too high
All of a sudden a big black puddin'
Came flyin' through the air
Wha saw the kilties comin'
Wha saw them gand awa'
Wha saw the kilties comin'
Sailin' doon the Broomielaw
Some o' them had tartan troosers
Some o' them had nane at a'
Some o' them had tartan troosers
Sailin' doon the Broomielaw.


A ring a ring o' roses
A cuppa cuppa shell
The duck's away to Hamilton
To buy a new bell
If you won't tak' it
I'll tak' it to masel
A ring a ring o' roses
A cuppa cuppa shell.


Salome, Salome, you should see Salome
Hands up there, skirts in the air
You should see Salome
Swing it, swing it
You should see her swing it
Hands up there, skirts in the air
You should see her swing it.

Old Rodger is dead and he's laid in his grave
laid in his grave, laid in his grave
Old Rodger is dead and he's laid in his grave
Ee aye laid in his grave

They planted an apple tree over his head
Over his head, over his head
They planted an apple tree over his head
Ee aye over his head

The apples got ripe and they all fell off
All fell off, all fell off
The apples got ripe and they all fell off
Ee aye they all fell off

There came an old woman a picking them up
A picking them up, a picking them up
There came an old woman a picking them up
Ee aye a picking them up

Old Rodger got up and gave her a kick
GHave her a kick, gave her a kick
Old Rodger got up and gave her a kick
Ee aye gave her a kick

It made the old woman go hippety hop
hippety hop, hippety hop
It made the old woman go hippety hop
Ee aye hippety hop.


Hard up kick the can
Mary Smith's got a man
If ye'd like to know his name
his name is Jimmy Thompson.

She'll be coming round the mountain when she comes
She'll be coming round the mountain when she comes
She'll be coming round the mountain
Coming round the mountain
Coming round the mountain when she comes

Singing I will if you will, so will I
Singing I will if you will, so will I
Singing I will if you will
I will if you will
I will if you will, so will I

She'll be riding six white horses when she comes
She'll be riding six white horses when she comes
She'll be riding six white horses
Riding six white horses
Riding six white horses when she comes

Singing I will if you will, so will I etc.

She'll be wearing silk pyjamas when she comes
She'll be wearing silk pyjamas when she comes
She'll be wearing silk pyjamas
Wearing silk pyjamas
Wearing silk pyjamas when she comes

Singing I will if you will, so will I etc.


Hot peas and barley–o, barley–o, barley–o
Hot peas and barley–o
Sugary cakes and candy
This is the way the teacher stands
This is the way she folds her arms
This is the way she claps her hands
And this is the way she dances.

The farmer wants a wife
The farmer wants a wife
Ee-o my daddy-o
The farmer wants a wife

The wife wants a child
The wife wants a child
Ee-o my daddy-o
The wife wants a child

The child wants a nurse
The child wants a nurse
Ee-o my daddy-o
The child wants a nurse

The nurse wants a dog
The nurse wants a dog
Ee-o my daddy-o
The nurse wants a dog

The dog wants a bone
The dog wants a bone
Ee-o my daddy-o
The dog wants a bone

The bone won't break
The bone won't break
Ee-o my daddy-o
The bone won't break.

The grand old duke of York
He had ten thousand men
He marched them up to the top of the hill
And he marched them down again
When they were up they were up
And when they were down they were down
And when they were only half way up
They were neither up nor down.


Two little sandy girls
Sitting on the shore
Crying weeping
Very very sore
Stand up Mary and wipe away your tears
And who's the one you love the best
And that's Lizzie dear.


My name is MacNamara
I'm the leader of the band
My wife is Betty Grable
She's the fairest in the land
She can dance and she can sing
And she can show a leg
The only thing she canni dae
Is fry ma ham and eggs
Ta ra ra ra, ta ra ra ra ra
The only thing she canni dae
Is fry ma ham and eggs.

We're the three wee galous girls
An' if ye'd like tae know
That if ye pick the fairest one
Ye'll have tae pick us a'
Wi' a rishy tishy petticoat
A rishy tishy o
Wi' a rishy tishy petticoat
A rishy tishy o


What is Rosie weeping for?
Weeping for, weeping for
What is Rosie weeping for?
All on a summer day

I'm weeping for my own true love
My own true love, my own true love
I'm weeping for my own true love
All on a summer day

Rise up and choose another love
Another love, another love
Rise up and choose another love
All on a summer day.


When grandmama met grandpapa
They danced the minuet
The minuet was too slow
They danced a quick step
With a chassy and a chassy
and a choo choo choo
A chassy and a chassy
And a choo choo choo
That's the way to do it.

Where are ye goin' ma bonnie wee lass?
Where are ye goin' ma dearie?
Where are ye goin' ma bonnie wee lass?
Ah'll have tae ask ma mammy

Hula Kadulaka, hula kadoo
Hula Kadulaka dandy
Hula Kadulaka, hula kadoo
Ah'll have tae ask ma mammy

Whit's yer name ma bonnie wee lass?
Whit's yer name ma dearie?
Whit's yer name ma bonnie wee lass?
Ah'll have tae ask ma mammy

Hula Kadulaka, hula kadoo
Hula Kadulaka dandy
Hula Kadulaka, hula kadoo
Ah'll have tae ask ma mammy.

Who'll buy the milk can?
The milk can, the milk can
Who'll buy the milk can?
Cock a leery-o

I'll buy the milk can
The milk can, the milk can
I'll buy the milk can
Cock a leery-o

Where will you get the money?
The money, the money
Where will you get the money?
Cock a leery-o

Sell father's feather bed
Feather bed, feather bed
Sell father's feather bed
Cock a leery-o

Where will father lie?
Father lie, father lie
Where will father lie?
Cock a leery-o

Lie in mother's bed
Mother's bed, mother's bed
Lie in mother's bed
Cock a leery-o

Where will mother lie?
Mother lie, mother lie
Where will mother lie?
Cock a leery-o

Lie in sister's bed
Sister's bed, sister's bed
Lie in sister's bed
Cock a leery-o

Where will sister lie?
Sister lie, sister lie
Where will sister lie?
Cock a leery-o

Lie in brother's bed
Brother's bed, brother's bed
Lie in brother's bed
Cock a leery-o

Where will brother lie?
Brother lie, brother lie
Where will brother lie?
Cock a leery-o

Lie in the pig sty
The pig sty, the pig sty
Lie in the pig sty
Cock a leery-o


Down in the jungle
Where nobody goes
A big fat mama
Sat a washing her clothes
With a rub a dub here
And a rub a dub there
That's the way she washes her clothes.

Who shaved the barber?
The barber, the barber
Who shaved the barber?
The barber shaved himself
Who put on his waistcoat?
His waistcoat, his waistcoat
Who put on his waistcoat?
He put it on himself
Catch him by the waistcoat
The jaicket, the overcoat
Tell him he's a billygoat
And throw him doon the stairs.


Water water wallflower
Growing up so high
We are all children
And we must all die
Except for Mary McCusker
The youngest of us all
For she can dance and she can sing
And she can dae the Heilin' fling
Fly, fly, fly, fly, fly
Turn your back to the wall again
Ye canni crack a biscuit
Ye canni smoke a pipe
Ye canni kiss yer wee laud
At ten o'clock at night
At ten o'clock at night
The moon shines bright
All the little angles
Dressed up in white.

Down in yonder meadow
Where the green grass grows
Where Mary Simpson
Bleaches all her clothes
She sang and she sang
And she sang so sweet
She sang Tommy Smith
Across the street
She huddled and she cuddled
And she sat upon his knee
Saying my dear Tommy
I hope you will agree
Mary made a dumpling
She made it awful nice
She cut it up in slices
And gave us all a slice
Saying taste it taste it
Don't say no
For tomorrow is my wedding day
And I must go.


Who'll come in to ma wee ring?
Ma wee ring, ma wee ring
Who'll come in to ma wee ring?
To make it a wee bit bigger

I'll come in to your wee ring
Your wee ring, your wee ring
I'll come in to your wee ring
To make it a wee bit bigger

Who'll come in to oor wee ring?
Oor wee ring, oor wee ring
Who'll come in to oor wee ring?
To make it a wee bit bigger

There came three Jews
Just new from Spain
To call upon my sister Jane
My sister Jane is far too young
I cannot bear her rattling tongue
So I'll away, away, away
And I'll come back another day
Come back, come back
Your choice to see
And who's the fairest one you see?
The fairest one that I can see
Is bonnie wee Lizzie
Will ye come to me?
Naw.
Ye dirty wee brat, ye widnae come
Ye widnae come, ye widnae come
Ye dirty wee brat, ye widnae come
Tae help me wi' ma washin'
Noo ah've got the Prince O' Wales
The Prince O' Wales, the Prince O' Wales
Noo ah've got the Prince O' Wales
Tae help me wi' ma washin'


Broken bridges falling down
Falling down, falling down
Broken bridges falling down
My fair lady

Here's the prisoner we have got
We have got, we have got
Here's the prisoner we have got
My fair lady.

## SECTION 3

## BALL GAMES

## INTRODUCTION

Ball game rhymes were chanted by the child as she bounced her ball against the wall and caught it. If she dropped the ball before the rhyme ended, she had to start at the beginning again.

If more than one child was playing, whoever finished the rhyme first was the winner.

Archibald bald bald
The King of the jews jews jews
Bought his wife wife wife
A pair of shoes shoes shoes
When the shoes shoes shoes
Began to wear wear wear
Archibald bald bald
Began to swear swear swear
When the swear swear swear
Began to stop stop stop
Archibald bald bald
Bought a shop shop shop
When the shop shop shop
Began to sell sell sell
Archibald bald bald
He went to hell hell hell.


As I went up the garden
I found a little farthing
I gave it to my mother
To buy a little brother
My brother was a sailor
He sailed across the sea
And all the fish that he could catch
Was one, two, three.


Mrs Brown went to town
With her knickers hanging down.

Are you going to golf sir?
No sir. Why sir?
Because I've got a cold sir.
Where did you catch the cold sir?
Up the North Pole sir.
What were you doing there sir?
Catching polar bears sir.
How many did you catch sir?
One two three four five
six seven eight nine ten.


Away up in Scotland
The land of the Scotch
There lives a wee lassie
I love very much
Her name is Susannah
But where is she now?
She's up in the highlands
A-milking the cow.


Bubble says the kettle
Bubble says the pot
Bubble bubble bubble
We are very hot
Shall I lift you off the fire
No, you needn't trouble
That is just the way we talk
Bubble bubble bubble.

Can can Caroline
washed her face in turpentine
Turpentine will make it shine
Can can Caroline.


Cobbler cobbler mend my shoe
have it done by half past two
Half past two is far too late
Have it done by half past eight.


Dan dan the funny wee man
Washed his face in the frying pan
Combed his hair with the leg of the chair
Dan dan the funny wee man.


Doctor doctor how's your wife
Very bad upon my life
Can she eat a bit of pie
Yes she can as well as I.


Down in Germany
This is what they say
Ikirikirasha I smell pasha
Down in Germany.

Here comes Mrs Macaroni
Riding on her big fat pony
Through the streets of Macaroni
This is Mary's washing day
Pom Pom Susie Anna
Pom Pom Susie Anna
Pom Pom Susie Anna
This is Mary's washing day.


I'm a little prairie flower
Growing wilder by the hour
Nobody wants to cultivate me
I'm as wild as wild can be.


I spent a' ma money on an old tin cuddy
But the old tin cuddy widnae go
So I took some sugarally
An' I hit on the belly
But the old tin cuddy widnae go.


Keyhole Kate from the Gallowgate
Died last night at half past eight
They put her in a coffin
She fell through the bottom
Keyhole Kate from the Gallogate

Madamoiselle went to town
Parlez vous
To buy herself a wedding gown
Parlez vous
And everybody in the town
Thought it was a lovely gown
Inky pinky parlez vous.


Mary McTavish sells fish
Three halfpence a dish
Cuts the heids aff
Cuts the heids aff
Mary McTavish sells fish.


Oh Mrs Docherty
Come tae bed alang wi' me
An' ah'll gie ye a cup o' tea
Tae make yer belly warm.


Kitsy Katesy had a canoe
It was yellow black and blue
Open the gates and let her through
That's Kitsy Katesy.


Mrs Red went to bed
In the morning she was dead.

Mrs MacLean she had a wee wean
An' she didnae know how tae nurse it
She gave it tae me
An' ah gave it some tea
An' it's bonnie wee belly bursted.


Mrs Simpson lives by the shore
She has daughters three and four
The eldest one is twenty four
Married to the boy next door.


Mrs White got a fright
In the middle of the night
She saw a ghost eating toast
Halfway up a lamp post.


Korky the cat thinks he's smart
Cos he put a penny
In the old man's hat
If you haven't got a penny
A ha'penny will do
If you haven't got a ha'penny
A farthing will do
If you haven't got a farthing
God bless you.

Now the war is over
And Hitler is dead
He wants to go to heaven
With a crown upon his head
But the Lord says no
He'll have to go below
There's only room for Churchill
And his wee banjo.


Old mother Reilly at the pawn shop door
A baby in her arms and a bundle on the floor
She asked for ten and she only got four
She nearly took the hinges off the pawn shop door


My mother's a queen
And my father's a king
I'm a little princess
And you're a dirty wee thing
It's not because you're dirty
It's not because you're clean
It's because you've got the chicken pox
And measles in between
If me mother knew
That I played with you
She'd put me over the bannister
And this is what she'd do
One two three o-leary
Four five six o-leary
Seven eight nine o-leary
Ten o-leary postman.

Queen Mary, Queen Mary
My age is sixteen
My father's a farmer in yonder green
He's plenty of money to dress me in silk
But there's nae bonnie laddie
Who'll tak' me awa'
Tak' me awa', tak' me awa'
There's nae bonnie laddie
Who'll tak' me awa'.


Rabbie Burns was born in Ayr
Now he stands in George's Square
If you'd like to see him there
Just jump on the bus and pay your fare
A penny, tuppence, thruppence
Fourpence, fivepence, sixpence
Sevenpence, eightpence, ninepence
Tenpence, elevenpence, a shilling


Salvation Army free from sin
Went to heaven in a corn mutton tin
The corn mutton tin began to smell
Salvation Army went to ...
Helensburgh Castle
Landed on a rock
The people passing by there
Got an awful shock.

Miss Polly had a dolly
Who was sick, sick, sick
So she called for the doctor
To come quick, quick, quick
The doctor came with his bag and his hat
And he knocked on the door
With a rat tat tat
He looked at the dolly and he shook his head
And he said Miss polly
Put her straight to bed
He wrote out a letter
For the pill, pill, pill
I'll be back in the morning
With a bill, bill, bill.


Early in the morning
Before eight o'clock
You should hear the postman knock
Up jumps Rosie
Running to the door
With a one a letter
Two a letter
Three a letter four.


Mrs McGuire sat in the fire
The fire was too hot
She sat in the pot
The pot was too wide
She sat in the Clyde
And a' the wee fishes
Ran up her backside.

Oliver Twist you can't do this
So what's the use of trying it?
If so, touch your toe
Through you go, big birly-oh.


Open the gates and let me in, sir
I am soaking to the skin, sir
Open the gates and let me in, sir
Early in the morning.


Pansy Potter the strong man's daughter
Went to school without her jotter
She got the belt, began to cry
Pansy Potter said goodbye.


P.K. Chewing gum, a penny a packet
First you chew it, then you crack it
Then you stick it to your jacket
P.K. Chewing gum a penny a packet.


Mary had a little lamb
She kept it in the lobbie
And every time a burgler came
It whistled for the bobby
Mary had a little lamb
She kept it in the scullery
A German bomb came whizzing down
And knocked the lamb to . . . .

Mary had a baby and she called him Sunny Jim
She put him in the bath tub
To see if he could swim
He drank all the water
He ate all the soap
He died last night
With a bubble in his throat.


Down in the jungle
Living in a tent
Better than a prefab
No rent.


Salvation Army free from sin
Went to heaven in a corn mutton tin
The corn mutton tin was made of brass
They all fell our and skint their ...
Ask no questions
Tell no lies
Keep your mouth shut
And you'll catch no flies.


Stop says the red light
Go says the green
Wait says the amber light
Blinking in between
That's what they say
And that's what they mean
We all must obey them
Even the Queen.

The big ship sails round the eely ally-o
The eely ally-o, the eely ally-o
The big ship sails round the eely ally-o
On the last day of September
The captain says we'll have to go below
Have to go below, have to go below
The captain says we'll have to go below
On the last day of September.


The big ship was leaving Bombay for today
Back to old Errin's Isle, so they say
Lizzie was standing with tears in her eyes
Along came Jimmy with two big black eyes
Saying 'Lizzie, oh Lizzie be mine, be mine
I'll send you a sweet valentine, valentine'
And he turned round and kissed her
And said he would miss her
Oh darling, it won't be for long.


The wind, the wind, the wind blows high
The rain comes tumbling from the sky
Rosie Speirs says she'll die
If she doesn't get the boy
With the big blue eye
Jimmie Quigley says he loves her
All the boys are fighting for her
She's the prettiest girl in Glasgow
Pray, pray, pray for her.

The pillar box is red and fat
His mouth is very wide
He wears a tammy on his head
It must be dark inside
And really it's the greatest thrill
When mother lets me stop
And post the letters one by one
I love to hear them drop.

Tommy had a gun and the gun was loaded
Tommy pulled the trigger and the gun exploded
No more Tommy, no more gun
No more damage to be done.

Up by the mountain
Down by the sea
Tommy broke a window
And he blamed it on me
Ah told my ma
My ma told my da
And Tommy got a hammerin'
Ha ha ha.

When I was young I had no sense
I thought I'd go to see
I stepped upon a Chinaman's ship
And this is what the Chinaman said to me
Up skalla, doon skalla,
Back skalla, roon skalla
That's what the Chinsman said to me.

Walter, Walter take me to the altar
I want to be a bridesmaid
Stamp Gibralter.


Wee Sam a piece on jam
Went to London in a pram
The pram broke what a joke
Wee Sam a piece on jam.


Where was Moses when the lights went out?
Up Sauchiehall Street smokin' a doubt
The doubt was wee and so was he
Where was Moses when the lights went out.


Yankee Doodle went to London
Riding on a pony
He stuck a feather in his hat
And called it Macaroni.


Over the garden wall
I let the baby fall
My mother came out
And gave me a clout
Over the garden wall.

## SECTION 4

## SKIPPING RHYMES

## INTRODUCTION

Skipping rope rhymes were sung as achild skipped with a skipping rope, either on her own or with two people at either end of the rope turning it for her as she skipped.

If her feet or dress caught in the rope before the rhyme had ended, she was'out' and would have to take her turn of turning or 'cawing' the rope for the others.

A house to let no rent to pay
Just ring the bell and run away
A house to let apply within
A lady put out for drinking gin
Gin you know is a very bad thing
So out pops Rosie and Mary comes in.


Bluebell cockle shell
Eevie ivie over
All in together this fine weather
Mother's in the kitchen
Doing her stitchin'
Baby's in the cradle
Playing with the ladle
One two three
And out goes she.

Horsie horsie don't you stop
Just let your feet go clippety clop
Your tail goes swish
And your wheels go round
Giddy up we're homeward bound.


I've a laudie in America
I've a laudie in Dundee i-ee i-ee
I've a laudie in Australia
And he's coming home
To marry me i-ee i-ee

First he took me to America
Then he took me to Dundee i-ee i-ee
Then he ran away and left me
With three bonnie babies
On my knee i-ee i-ee

One was sitting by the fireside
One was sitting on my knee i-ee i-ee
One was sitting at the doorstep
Shouting daddy, daddy, daddy
Come to me i-ee i-ee.


Chinese government
Black man's daughter
Tra la la a very good sign
Wind blows high down from the sky
In goes Lizzie wi' the big black eye

On a mountain stands a lady
Who she is I do not know
All she wants is gold and silver
All she wants is a fine young man
So I call in Rosie dear, Rosie dear
Rosie dear
So I call in Rosie dear
And out pops Lizzie till the next new year.


Please keep off the grass
To let the ladies pass
Here comes the policeman
Riding on his a..
Ask no questions
Tell no lies
Keep your mouth shut
And catch no f..
Fly away Peter, fly away Paul
Come back Peter, Come back P..
Polly in the kitchen
Doing a little stitching
In comes the bogie man
And out pops she.

Vote vote vote for Rosie Speirs
In comes Lizzie at the door
Lizzie is the one that we all love the best
So we don't want Rosie any more, shut the door.


There she goes, there she goes
Peery heels and pointed toes
Look at her feet
She think she's neat
Black stockings and dirty feet.


Step the gaily on we go
Heel for heel and toe for toe
Arm in arm and row in row
All for Jeannie's wedding.

Teddy bear, teddy bear touch the ground
Teddy bear, teddy bear turn right around
Teddy bear, teddy bear go upstairs
Teddy bear, teddy bear say you prayers
Teddy bear, teddy bear turn off the light
Teddy bear, teddy bear say goodnight.


Granny's in the kitchen
Doing a little stitchin'
In pops the bogie man
And out pops she.


Christopher Columbus was a very brave man
He sailed o'er the ocean in an old tin can
And the waves grew higher and higher and over
One two three four five six
Seven eight nine and ten.

# SECTION 5

# ELIMINATION GAMES

## INTRODUCTION

Elimination rhymes were used to see who would be 'het' at a game.

One person recited the rhyme whilst pointing to the others in turn as she spoke each word.

Whoever she was pointing at when the rhyme ended was eliminated. The rhyme was repeated with one person less each time. Whoever was last to be eliminated was 'het'.

An aeroplane an aeroplane
An aeroplane to watch the wean
An' see ma daddy comin' hame.


A penny o' chips
To grease your lips
You are out
If you had been where ah had been
Ye widnae hae been put out
Wha buy ma celery?
Wha buy ma leek?
Wha buy ma bonny wee lass
Wi' the red rosie cheek?
You are out.


As I was walking down the street
I saw a scabby donkey
I one it, you two it,
I three it, you four it,
I five it, you six it,
I seven it, you ate it.


Cinderella dressed in yellow
Went upstairs to kiss her fellow
How many kisses did she get? Five
One two three four five
You are out.

Big O wee O bouncing B
The cat's in the cupboard
An you can't catch me.


Dic dic tation corporation
How many buses are in the station
Close your eyes and think of a lucky number.
Five. One two three four five
You are out.


Each peach pear plum
I spy Tom Thumb
Tom Thumb in the wood
I spy Robin Hood
Robin Hood in the cellar
I spy Cinderella
Cinderella at the ball
I spy Henry Hall
Henry Hall at his house
I spy Mickey Mouse
Mickey Mouse in his cradle
I spy Betty Grable
Betty Grable is a star
S-T-A-R you are out.


Scotland, England, Ireland, Wales
All tied up in monkeys tails
You are out.

Eachy peachy pay a plum
Pitchin' tatties up the lum
Santa Claus got one on the bum
You are out.


Eenty teenty number nine
Dip your nose in turpentine
Turpentine will make it shine
Eenty teenty number nine.


Eeny meeny miny mo
Sit the baby on the po
When he's done wipe his bum
And throw the paper up the lum.


Eeny meeny macka racka
Em oh dominacka
Alla backa sugaracka
Om pom push.


Eeny meeny miny mo
Catch a nipper by the toe
If he squeals let him go
Eeny meeny miny mo.

Eerie oarie roon the table
Eerie oarie out
If ye're able eat the table
You are out.


Hide and go seek
Yer mother's a leek
Yer faither's a cabbage
An' you're a wee sneak
Who'll buy the cabbage?
Who'll buy the leek?
Who'll buy the bonnie wee lass
Wi' the red rosie cheeks? .
You are out.


Hokey pokey yankee fun
How dae ye like yer tatties done?
First in brandy then in rum
That's how I like my tatties done.


If a bumbee stung a bumbee
On a bumbee's bum
What colour would the bumbee's bum be
Red. R-E-D spells red
And red you must have on
You are out.

If I'm daft, you're silly
I'm the man and your the cuddy
A cuddy walks on four legs
And I walk on two
And the last cuddy I saw
Was very like you.


I found. Is it black?
Or is it brown
Or is it like
A half a crown.


I spy with my little eye
A little girl with 'B' in her eye
'B' stands for Bella
Bonnie wee Bella
She shall have a baby
Dressed in Navy
Hop hop hop to the butcher's shop.


Wee Ikey pow wow
Very fond of chow wow
Wee Ikey sugarally
Wee Ikey oo
He go to Hong Kong
Whitey manny came along
And stole a little doggie
From the wee Chinee.

I think, I think I smell a stink
Coming from Y–O–U.


Wee Jeannie Ink fell down the sink
Guess what colour the blood was
Red. R–E–D spell red and red you must have on
You are out.


Johnnie and Lizzie up a tree
K–I–S–S–I–N–G
First comes love
Then comes marriage
Then comes a baby
In a wee tin carriage.

My mother and your mother
Were hanging out some clothes
My mother gave your mother
A punch on the nose
Guess what colour the blood will be
Close your eyes and think, think, think
Blue. B–L–U–E spells blue
And blue you must have on
If you have this colour on
Please step right out of this
G–A–M–E spells game
And O–U–T spells out
With a dirty washing clout
Right over your face
Just like that.


One potato, two potato
Three potato, four
Five potato, six potato
Seven potato more.


One two sky blue
All out, but you.


One two three four five six seven
All good children go to heaven
When they die their sins forgiven
One two three four five six seven.

Oor wee Jeannie
Wi' the nice clean peeny
Guess what colour it was?
Pink. P-I-N-K spells pink
And pink you must have on
You are out.


Plum pudding, apple tart
Tell me the name of your sweethart
John. J-O-H-N spells John
You are out.


One two three four
Jenny at the cottage door
Eating cherries off a plate
Five six seven eight.


There's a party on the hill
Will you come, come, come
Bring your own cup and saucer
And your own cream bun
Mary will be there with a ribbon in her hair
Guess what colour the ribbon will be
Blue. B-L-U-E spells blue
And blue you must have on
You are out.

ELIMINATION RHYMES

This year, next year
Sometime, never
You are out.


Three wee tatties in a pot
Take one oot an' see if it's hot
If it's hot, cut it's throat
Three wee tatties in a pot.